Dreams And Reality

Dreams to be remembered and reality of life.

D. Farris

BookLeaf Publishing

India | USA | UK

Dedication

To the sister's god gave me, Cat and Amber and my
husband, Henry.
Without you this would not have been possible.

Preface

Some events in this book really occurred, others are dreams that I have had. This is a mixture of reality and dreams that has either happened personally or has came up in a dream. My goal is to ensure that people of all walks of life can enjoy this or even relate to the poems in this book.

Acknowledgements

I would like to Acknowledge Cat Puente for pushing me to do this, encouraging me, and keeping an upbeat attitude.
Without her I would not have been able to get the opportunity to go on this beautiful journey.

I would like to acknowledge Amber Morris for encouraging me and reminding me that I am capable of doing this. For being hard on me and pushing me past bounds that I didn't know I had.

I would like to acknowledge my daughter, La'Lanie Boston, for the beautiful book cover that she created for me. May your art take you far in life.

Last but not least, my husband who provided me with the quiet space to work on this beautiful book and gave me ideas for the poems to write when I had writers block.

1. Dream

Dream a little dream,
Can you imagine the scene,
Perfect sky's and green grass,
The smell of rain as it just passed,
Smiles all around with hearts filled full of joy,
The children sitting down playing with a toy,
A couple on a picnic and two fishing buddies at the
pond,
Looking all around seeing everyone bond,
An elderly couple sitting on a bench talking and holding
hands,
The teenage girls that's all out getting their tans,
The teenage boys that playing football just for sport,
The quiet guy that is nervous to court,
It is a perfect little dream that we all wish to have,
But the imagination gives us that to bask,
So dream the little dreams and make it reality,
No one's dreams is just a formality.

2. Finding His Way

His mind is running a marathon trying to figure out life,
He doesn't get it as he has the kids, the house, and the
wife,
But he feels like a piece of him is missing within,
So he tries to go out and hang with some friends,
That doesn't help and he is still empty inside,
Deep within it feels like he has died,
So he takes to substances to try to get away,
That doesn't help so he goes and works longer hours
each day,
Still a missing piece that he hasn't figured out,
He keeps trying to take all the different routes,
He finally falls apart and seeks the help that he needs,
The trauma that he endured as child still proceeds,
He started learning things about himself that he
otherwise would not,
Now his healing journey cannot even be stopped,
He learns how to express and cut people out,
He learns how to love himself and stop with the doubt,

That's what its like to love yourself,
Never dim your light for anyone else.

3. The Way Home

The sky was dark and lighting all around,
No rain or thunder or even a sound,
She walked through the desert of pitch-black sand,
With just a water bottle in her hand,
She came across a creature so mighty and strong,
But was gentle as he asked her what's wrong,
I am lost and have no way to find my home,
I am scared and I feel all alone,
He smiled and said I can help get you where you need to
go,
But you have to go through three tests to first help you
grow,
The first you will find is easy to do,
You must stir and then drink this brew,
What is in it? she asked with suspicion,
Don't ask any questions and listen,
So she stirred the brew and drank it down,
She felt funny and expressed a frown,
Sleep he said as you need it for part two,
She couldn't help it even though she feared what he

might do,
Waking from a slumber she noticed he was gone,
In his place a letter about a smidgen long,
She must get through the city without being seen,
There are hungry creatures that are the size of a
wolverine,
She went through the city and almost got caught,
Now she is at the end and feeling so fraught,
The creature comes to her and says she has one more
task,
She must endure the pulling buildings of her future and
past,
One will get her home and the other will keep her there,
She must figure out which one and be aware,
he chained her wrists to the tall buildings and told her
good luck,
She guess she chose right because that's when she woke
up.

4. Conversation with Death

Sitting in a chair at a table all alone,
Looking at him but there is no face to be known,
Just a black cloak with gold on the trim,
The black mist surrounding making the body look dim,
No eyes that are seen or sound from his mouth,
But he could still be understood even without,
His excitement could be felt as he spoke in my mind,
Telling me how everything works and when it's
someone's time,
The strings of someone's life dims and fades,
And he hovers around as he aids,
Helping them get from one path to the next,
As their memory fades from the life they just left,
He said his turn is ending and he can finally be at peace,
Someone else will take his place and he will be released.

5. Forbidden Love

Her hair long and black with skin as pale as snow,
He knows what she is but his heart continues to grow,
Rainy and wet stuck in the same place,
Days on an end he continues to see her face,
So stoic so he knows she been through pain,
He has too as even his marriage is in vain,
She's a good wife and even better cook,
But she is boring like an old dusty book,
This woman that has captivated his heart and mind,
She's more like a man's favorite food with fine wine,
Her brothers though won't let anyone near,
Acting like she's sick for only out of fear,
But when his wife is finally sound asleep,
He moves through the house so that they can meet,
He doesn't know his wife pretends and then follows him
each night,
Until they were found by the brothers which ensued a
fight,
His wife came running and right before him turned
twice his size,

On all four paws ready for war with all the guys,
The oldest of the brothers took a step forward and asked
for a meet,
She shimmered into human and walked away with them
to speak,
Him and the other woman stood there with no sound,
Waiting for the verdict to come back around,
When they returned none looked pleased with the
outcome,
The wife spoke first and said what was to be done,
She said since you shown you were never mine,
I then release you from this marriage bind,
Then one of the brothers spoke and said you must
change him if he is to be with us,
So make your choice go and discuss,
She went to him spoke softly and bit him on the neck,
Then they all disappeared while the wife wept and wept,
That was the last they were seen by anyone ever again,
That was the story the wife gave to the ten councilmen.

6. Get Back to Us

Can we just talk about the problems that exist,
instead of treading through them like it's a mist,
we used to have late night conversations about
everything,
now it's like we don't talk about anything,
tell me you still love me and we can work through this,
because out of everything I lost its me and you I miss,
we started life together but so far apart,
and every time I bring it up you say don't start,
I'm not trying to argue about our relationship,
I'm just trying to get back to that courtship,
Where we made time for each other,
But now we are just stuck in this slumber,
Of doing our daily life repetitively,
Sitting on this love so negatively,
I miss so much about us,
But now its like all we do is fuss,
So can we stop this mess and love again?,
Can we go back to how we used to love then?

7. Truckers Wife

Long road to go to get back home to her,
Driving down this highway and everything becoming a
blur,
About to fall asleep behind this big truck wheel,
What's keeping me going is her intoxicating feel,
She's the realist one in my life,
That's why I made her my wife,
She accepts me just for who I am,
And her cooking makes me go damn,
All I'm thinking about is getting home and showing her
some love,
She makes my heart fly so high above,
Understanding of my career,
On top of that she got that severe,
Being a trucker's wife is not for the weak,
And to top it off her love is so sweet.

8. Narcassistic Abuse

I was a soft-spoken girl when we first met,
Then here you come and it was like it was Russian
roulette,
You wanted to play games and cheat and lie,
And I wanted someone who wouldn't say goodbye,
Then you decided that the game needed to be physical,
And everything about us became very critical,
Driving crazy down the highway and saying you're
going to kill us,
Me looking at you with fear but also disgust,
We had those babies in the car when you threatened to
take us out,
To threaten their lives like that I don't know what it was
about,
Maybe it was the control that you wanted over us so bad,
And trying to get away without us getting hurt was so
sad,
Body slamming me to the ground while I protect these
kids from your wrath,
Trying to figure out how to get us out and going over

that math,
Kids locking their door and me running to the bathroom to hide,
You putting holes in the wall while I sat there and cried,
Son going to the ER over getting spanked and falling on a razor blade,
Me rushing home to get him to go the hospital both mad and afraid,
But somehow you blamed me through all your mess,
Had your mom agree that I was behind your stress,
Yet I was the one working and scared to come to the house,
Trying to play with our daughter while being as quiet as a mouse,
You validating your cheating like if I was just this or that,
Acting as if you were the king and I was to be the joker with the hat,
Getting you a job and seeing if you would leave us for another,
Then finally through it all you found the other,
Supply that you were to use and it was such a relief,
But to ensure our safety I had to act like I was in grief,
Even though the ones you hurt the most was these beautiful amazing kids,
And in the long run it will be you who they are rid.

9. The Little Lost Bear

Tiny little fluffy bear walking along the creek,
Looking for maybe a fish or two so that he can eat,
Hearing a twig snap on the other side,
Him getting scared and eyes going wide,
Then out pops his friend with a smile on her face,
I brought some honey do you want a taste,
He sits besides her and takes the jar in his paws,
Some going in his tummy and some going down his
jaws,
She saved him from the fire and put him in a new place,
This place he now calls home is the perfect embrace.
Lots of woods and a pond with fresh fish every day,
She even brings jars of honey and will stay to play,
His siblings and mom he has not seen since the fire,
Seeing them again is something he would desire,
But he knows that it may not happen as they all split up,
He was running then picked up and put in a tub,
They gave him something and he fell into a deep sleep,
Next thing he knew he was in a forest so deep,
Not like his home where he could roam around free,

It was a stopping point where he was unable to be,
I have a surprise for you the girl said with glee,
In fact its not just one surprise but three,
Then three guys came out with cages covered around,
He took a step back scared to even make a sound,
The cover was lifted and the cages opened wide,
Out came his siblings and his heart filled with pride,
They all started talking at once and filled full of joy,
Then he told them about the girl who brings honey and
funny toys,
He told them how much fish is sitting in the pond,
And they told him that they lost their mom,
He cried a good cry for days on end,
But the girl kept coming out never giving up on being
his friend.

10. Spiritual Warfare

Out in a field with green grass and woods all around,
It was just me and a red truck with a booming sound,
The booming sound said a war is coming quick get in the
truck,
I hear a shotgun sound and quickly duck,
Get in the truck the booming sound said again,
I snapped I'm trying to but I can't get in,
The doors are locked and the window is up,
There is only the tiny window sitting at the front,
Silence is what I received but I felt the disappointment,
Yet at the same time I felt his anointment,
I tried one more time and with a hanger got the window
down,
As the clouds turned into a greyish brown,
Quick jump in the truck the booming voice said,
I did as I was told without a thought in my head,
Waking up from the dream was so surreal,
And then I got that call which gave me the reveal,
She finally snapped and they want her in a facility,
They said she is not well mentally,

So I said give me just a moment I'm on my way,
While driving got a text from my dad saying it'll be okay,
Got her to the hospital and she told it all,
How they abused her and she finally had her fall,
Got her home and set up with a therapist,
Knowing that her journey is so delicate,
A spiritual warfare that became a physical fight,
But she knows now everything will be alright.

11. Three Snakes

Three snakes a warning,
Foretold the next morning,
Two red snakes and sometimes one black,
Coming in for the kill just to attack,
Either screaming or fighting depending on the dream,
The black one I thought was with me but he was just
mean,
Waiting for the red ones to go ahead and bite,
Curling up next to me for the underhanded fight,
Mostly three being red and I know what that entails,
But when that black one bites it leaves some bloody
trails,
The red snakes I can handle but that black one draws me
in,
How it seems so comforting but it is only playing
pretend,
These are the warnings that come before the storms,
And its like they all stand in a form,
First red snake is the ex and his people raising trouble,
Tearing me and the kids down from our little healing

bubble,
Then here comes the mom with her leave her she's the
devil mess,
Saying "my son should obey me even if your married"
nevertheless,
Then the third snake oh it could be out of three,
They tend to go back and forth taking turns to see,
Which one can try to cause chaos because that is what
they like,
Even though he is my husband and I am his wife,
Now that black snake gets me every time,
Because I have the thought of I am his and he is mine,
But that second and third red snake keeps coming into
play,
And instead of having my back the loyalty goes away,
Surrounded by a ton of them but only three red snakes
tend to bite,
But sometimes that black one causes me to back up and
have to fight,
The three warning from those dreams,
Always gives me a heads up and shows me not all is
what it seems.

12. The Old Lady

Sitting by the fire watching the waves of the ocean,
When a lady came up trying to hand me a potion,
Drink it she said and you will have all the riches you
desire,
I looked at her and said now we all know you are a liar,
She said you never know there might be something that
catches your eye,
Yeah no I replied I think I would rather die,
So she left but said she would be back sometime soon,
And there she was right in the market at noon,
Can't I just shop without this crazy old lady,
She replied if you take the drink then yeah maybe,
I asked her what's in it for her if she is pressuring for
this drink,
She looked at me and said ill be broken from a link,
A link of what and will I then be attached,
She said you are strong that's why you would be a good
match,
That still doesn't answer my question now tell me what
you mean,

She looked at me and said don't you want to be seen,
I could care less about that now go away,
Since you won't answer my questions you can find
another fool to play,
Then she used a force throw me far and wide,
And when I landed I opened my eyes,
I was back on my bed confused for a minute,
The reality felt dream that was in zenith.

13. Gone for Good

You hated me from birth until I became an adult,
Then it was me you turned to for consult,
I forgave you for the hate that you gave,
Then you started coming down sick in waves,
So many times in and out of the hospital,
Every single time was an ICU submittal,
But you made it out even with all your health,
It was like your body fought and had so much stealth,
Until that one day of the hospital stay,
That made you forever go away,
You trusted me enough to give me control,
and I took it serious with every part of my soul,
I advocated hard to keep you here,
But I understand you was tired and wanted to leave,
And now here I am on the journey to grieve,
So tops up to you and the strength that you had,
Don't worry I'll take care of dad.

14. Dream Hopping

The night was clear with the sky full of stars,
He looked at me and said do you know where we are?,
No I said but I will follow you where you will go,
He took my hand and smiled ever so slow,
Then we jumped into the water that crispy clear,
But when I came up he was nowhere near,
The scene was different and it was a pool,
With the sun shinning and the air a little cool,
Like as if I was in the body but had no control,
She walked to someone I knew but didn't know,
Giving him a kiss and picking up a book,
And when looking up another scene had took,
Back in the woods by a fire burning bright,
He looked at me and said you gave me a huge fright,
You hit your head on a rock and I pulled you out,
Made sure you was ok after giving you mouth to mouth,
But we must go soon before they find us,
I already checked you did not concuss,
Then I heard mom as I was awaken by my child,
Yep that dream was little weird and wild.

15. Life Change

Trying to catch his breath,
Running from the people that wishes his death,
Lost in a city he doesn't know and trying to hang tight,
He was doing some things that he knew wasn't right,
It caught up to him pretty fast,
Now he is running group in masks,
He knew he shouldn't have snuck in to this place,
Then all he seen covered was face after face,
He seen to much and now they was all out for blood,
His to be precise and now he's stuck in this flood,
Of people that he can't escape,
Because he can only run so far as he is out of shape,
He ducked into a building he knew nothing about,
As these people are out there looking for him like a
scout,
Come young man he heard from behind,
He stopped and turned scared out of his mind,
The old lady grabbed his hand walking him further in
the place,
Why don't you tell me what's going on and maybe you

can stay,
So he explained to her about his day,
She said you can stay but on one condition,
You must serve the homeless and go on missions,
You must also stop your mischief and listen,
Agreed he said I learned my lesson,
So he lived his days in solitude and there was no more
stressin.

16. Girl and Wolf

Listening to her music jamming away,
Not realizing that her life is about to go astray,
She just got promoted and the day was going smooth,
So she treated herself and sat down in a booth,
Ordered her a burger with some fries and shake,
And then there it went the big earthquake,
No not the kind that shakes the ground,
The kind that comes when someone comes around,
He slid smoothly in her booth and took a big sniff,
And his eyes so grey that she could get lost in that bliss,
She took the courage to speak her mind,
Even though this wolf was just so dang fine,
Who are you and what do you want,
Can't I enjoy a beautiful girl in this restaurant,
No you cannot now speak or leave,
I cant leave without you as its time for your retrieve,
I wont go and I'm out I already made that clear,
And you wont try to bully me or make me fell fear,
Im not doing anything but letting you enjoy your food,
But your father is outside and he is not in the mood,

She froze burger halfway to her mouth,
I have to go and I have to find a way out,
Don't worry sweet cheeks all the exits are blocked,
She stood up looking around in shock,
Fine I'll go but you just signed my ending,
No sweet cheeks but our marriage is pending,
She passed out and he caught her before she hit the
ground,
And when she woke up to him she had already been
bound.

17. One Light Town

Late at night riding around,
In this little bitty one light town,
Driving down to the square,
All the young ones party there,
Trying to have a good time,
Seeing who can be the most to outshine,
Taking that car up and down the strip,
Showing off to see who has the best whip,
Just a Friday night in a one light town,
Having fun and getting down,
Sitting in the back of the truck with the blanket out,
Looking at the stars and figuring out what life is about,
Back to a more simple time,
When everything was more like fine wine,
Man those days will be missed,
To that one light town I blow a goodbye kiss.

18. A Trip in a Day

Driving along down a desert highway,
Listening to music doing it my way,
Kids bickering back and forth,
That travel going towards north,
Life not happening like we expected,
But even then we are all connected,
Making it to our destination with speed,
Six hour trip that was suppose to be eight,
Dealing with calls that I so much hate,
Communicating with people that I don't even like,
But its not about me so I gotta do this right,
Finally making it to my final destination,
So that I can finally get that information,
Traveling on back and hightailing it back to my home,
So I can finally be alone.

19. Toddler

Little bitty feet that pitter patter so fast,
The smile with the little cute laugh,
Joy all around and the world so bright,
Not one single thing can cause a fright,
From here to there and all around,
There is so much to explore and a lot to be found,
Mind full of wonders that can help so much,
So many different things to touch,
Everything looks either small or big,
Going outside to the dirt and beginning to dig,
Wondering how things taste or even smell,
Listening to noises like a small bell,
Toddler life is so full of wonder,
Even when there are tons of no's from the mother.

20. A Message in a Dream

Getting out of a truck and going in a car shop.
There is this guy and girl speaking another language
nonstop,
Got thrown some bread from two randoms that
disappeared,
Inside the shop the man was acting weird,
He went up these steps and came back down,
Then he turned away and turned back around,
With it strapped to his chest everything went boom,
Then I switch to walking on a dirt road mind full of
doom,
No shoes and thirsty thinking I'm not going to make it,
Then I see a house on a farm and made my way lickety
split,
Make to the house and no one is there,
But then a red truck pulls up and I felt the care,
She hops out and asks if I was okay,
I looked and said water and I began to sway,
She had me sit down and handed me a water bottle,
I drank it down so fast it was like full throttle,

Then we see black cars coming down the road,
She told her kids to go in as the vehicles slowed,
A guy got out and told her some news,
She broke down crying and he went to diffuse,
Once he was done he looked over at me,
Said everything would be alright even though I didn't
see,
Then he said he would give me his number but I
probably wouldn't call,
I woke up then and I remember it all.

21. Welcome to America

Do you ever wonder where the beauty is that was most
promised,
Reaching out for the picket fences and the life that was
supposed to be honest,
But all we got are lies told and expect us to conform,
Instead we are stuck in a state of mourn,
Calling it the land of the free but its only free for the
rich,
The rest of us are modern day slaves that they try to
keep split,
Can't say this or even do that,
Can't go on a certain little app,
Now there is nothing that will keep us from going
insane,
All because they want to control in vain,
Wondering what happened to not price gouging and
control,
Where we were told that we are a nation as a whole,
But our voices no longer have movement,
And they expect this to be the improvement,

Our voices are cut short and thoughts don't matter,
Bow down to the old guys and only robots are a factor,
Keep our heads down or it's the disappearance of self,
Because all that matters is keeping the wealthy in
wealth,
Take us out early and only make chemical foods
affordable,
While they get the good stuff while driving their
convertible,
Then if you try to leave you have to have lots of money
to get away,
So it's stuck in modern day slavery and being fully
betrayed,
Then tell us to have kids to be stuck in this cycle of
destruction,
All so they can have a good life and we can help them
function,
Then tell us to hush and sit down obey what they say,
And if we fight back then we are put on display,
As a sacrificial lamb to scare everyone who dares,
Because as they see it we are just properties of theirs,
Welcome to America where its home of the slaves,
Where it's torture and death for those who misbehaves.